"I Don't Know Why They're Bothering, You're Going to Die Anyways"

(A Story of Survival)

Linda Ruiz

Contents

Dedication   IV

Introduction   V

1. ONCE UPON AN ACCIDENT   1

2. A LOOK BACK AT CHILDHOOD   11

3. A FRESH COAT OF PAINT   15

4. A TARGET ON MY BACK   19

5. CALLING OUT (SOME OF) THE CREEPS   22

6. THE DIFFERENCE RESPECT MAKES   32

7. NOW I'M THE BOSS   39

8. I SURVIVED...AND I KEEP ON SURVIVING   43

This book is dedicated to my amazing mother Hilda who has never stopped believing in me. Your prayers and strong faith in Jesus have sustained me and helped make me stronger in my own faith. I also dedicate this to the three babies (though each are strong, adult women now). Laura, Jennifer, and Christina, you are the best sisters in the world and my love for you stretches to the highest heights, like a tall totem pole that reaches to heaven. In my eyes you are perfect and can do no wrong!

Introduction

I was around 20 years-old when I had the *audacity*, as some may see it, to enter a male dominated field: the construction trade. I hadn't planned on pursing a career in construction, namely as a painter, yet the opportunity fell into my lap, and I took hold of it. At the time, I was in need of a decent paying job and, besides, I've never been one to sit behind a desk. It was as simple as that. So I entered the world of dusty, busy construction sites, chauvinistic men, messy paint cans, and heavy equipment without knowing then of the on-going and often traumatic events and challenges I would face as a woman in this field. It was obvious from day one that I was not welcomed in this "man's world." I stuck with it, though, and learned my trade well. You'll discover through my story the rough road I've travelled--often a hell of a journey--and I'll share with you some of what I've learned as a result.

I've suffered physically and emotionally, mostly at the hands of men, but I'm healing. I'm overcoming ... and that, too, is a process. As I've continued in my journey, I've proved others wrong and proved to myself that I am worthy of respect and of life itself . Not only have I survived the abuse and other injustices that have too often invaded my life, but I've been able to rise above them. I've also learned from my own mistakes. No one is infallible--we all make them. I can say, though, that today I am an older and wiser survivor! And I eventually rose up to establish my own thriving business in this "man's world" of construction. I succeeded.

I'm writing my story now to inspire, encourage, and empower other women who find themselves struggling as they work and navigate life in male-dominated industries or circumstances. You don't have to become or stay a victim. If you are being victimized or feel threatened that you will be, you can change your course. You have more power than you think. Not only can you survive, you can succeed and even thrive. You have a say and a voice, and I hope this book helps you find it.

1

ONCE UPON AN ACCIDENT

It Happened on the 4th of July

Lying there on the gurney in the hospital elevator, I saw it: a bright light. Something unlike anything I had ever seen before. Isn't this what others at death's door have reported? *Something supernatural? Jesus?* My experience is more proof that such a light exists. I was on my way out, leaving this world...nearly gone. Though I was unconscious, I saw that light and it was then that I heard the hospital attendant standing next to me say words that continue to ring in my ear these 40-plus years later: "I don't know why they're bothering," he said, as he rode with me in the elevator, transporting me to another floor for treatment. "You're going to die anyways." (An aunt of mine later confirmed those words as she had been told that as well, that I wasn't going to make it.) The bright light then disappeared and, just like that, I was no longer heavenbound. I would soon learn that I was actually entering a type of hell, in many respects--a journey that had begun earlier in the day.

I had been in a terrible accident. I'd later learn that my injuries, though surprisingly not fatal, would be drastically life-altering. The accident caused 23 fractures in my face, demolishing it. My teeth were knocked out. I was bloody and bruised. My body was broken in several places as well--ribs busted, my right wrist snapped. I'd been given a tracheotomy. Lying on that gurney, I was in a tremendous amount of pain and fell in and out of consciousness from the intensity of it. No doubt the sight of me had to be horrible-like something out of a tragic horror movie. As my near-lifeless body lay there, I couldn't talk, but my ears functioned just fine. I was still a human being with an innate will to fight for life. God had made the choice to keep me on earth and was giving me a second chance. It was a miracle. I was a miracle! Still, those words uttered in that hospital elevator stung me and I'm sure they will for the rest of my life. *You don't know why they're bothering? Why is he saying that? Am I not worth the bother?*

It was July 4, 1979. Before the accident, it had been a typical summer day in Texas. Of course, it was sweltering outside, but I had lived in this Longhorn State long enough to handle the heat. I was in my early twenties at the time and this was a holiday--a day off work and a chance to relax and have some fun. I was ready for a break. My work was very physical and tiring and there seemed to be constant conflicts which took a toll on me emotionally I didn't have solid plans to celebrate the Fourth so when I was invited to a male co-worker's house for a barbeque, I agreed to come. He told me at the time that other co-workers would be there. So I thought it would be a smart move on my part to attend the barbeque and be part of the group. As a woman working in such an extremely male-dominated business as construction, I felt that I had to do what I could to fit in and make these guys accept me. Acceptance was key. Acceptance could lead to respect and respect would make my working environment less stressful and threatening.

I was an apprentice painter when I met this man who had invited me to his house (I refer to him now as "Heathen" because he is unworthy of being called by his true name). I'd been assigned through the Painter's Union to be his helper when I was first starting out. He was quite a bit older than me, but we had become friends, or so I thought. Sometimes Heathen would take me to lunch. We would talk. He'd try to impress me with how successful he was, showing me his bank books and bragging about the money he had. I really didn't care, but It didn't bother me to listen, and it seemed to please him to have someone to show off to. Insecure people, I've learned, feel compelled to magnify themselves.

While I was working as his apprentice, my need for a car became more and more apparent. I was used to taking the bus, but I had had a particularly unsettling experience when I was dropped off at a bus stop in a dangerous part of town, quite far from the hospital job site where I was currently working. I told Heathen about the fear I felt and ended up asking him if he'd be willing to help me buy a car of my own so I wouldn't have to depend on the bus. Being dropped off a distance from job sites and in undesirable neighborhoods had happened more than once. He agreed to loan me the money for a down payment on a car. I sincerely appreciated his generosity, but I came to learn, in a near-fatal way, that there were strings attached.

Just a week after Heathen loaned me the money, I was given a different assignment by the Union. They sent me to work for another painter which meant I would no longer be working for Heathen. I hadn't put in this request to change job sites, but it probably looked to him as if I had--like I was trying to avoid him--and I was sure he wasn't happy about it. Still, as an apprentice, I answered to the Union so I had to go where they assigned me. I ended up running into Heathen some time later and that's when he invited me to his house on July 4th. Another reason to accept the invitation to his barbeque was that I figured it would help appease any grudge he may be harboring toward me. I had continued to make my car payments and repay his loan, and I wasn't avoiding him. Attending his little gathering on July 4th would help him to see that.

When I arrived at his place in Bandera, about 40 miles from San Antonio, I was surprised to find him there alone. *Where are the other painters? He told me they would be here.* It didn't take long before I realized that there would be no other painters coming to his Fourth of July "party," and I began to feel uneasy. I asked him about it, and he muttered some excuses and handed me a beer. We talked and after a while he brought out some chicken from the kitchen. *Not much of a barbeque.* I hung out for a while, but as I became more and more uncomfortable in his presence I felt instinctively like I needed to get out of there. I asked him if I could use his phone and call my cousins who lived in San Antonio. I have a big family, and I knew that some were probably gathering for the holiday. At that point I just wanted to get away from Heathen. As I went to the other room to make the call and let my family know I'd be coming, I left my opened beer can in the living room. I'm sure Heathen had to have heard my conversation and knew I planned to take off. I rejoined him after my call and finished my beer (I had only had the one) before I announced I was leaving. But as I walked through the kitchen on my way outside, I felt strange. I stumbled. I became so dizzy that I had to grab hold of the kitchen counter to steady myself I didn't realize it at the time, but Heathen had slipped acid into my drink (this fact was discovered later when I was in the hospital and my mom was told I had acid in my system. I hadn't taken any acid. The only way the drug was in my system was that it had been slipped into my drink). Determined to leave, I told myself I was feeling well enough to drive, but I don't remember getting into my car. The next thing I remember, I was in the hospital.

The pieces of what happened between the moment I left Heathen's house and waking up in the hospital came together, in part, later for me. It turns out that as I drove away from his place I hit a boulder and flipped my car on a desolate road. I wasn't wearing my seatbelt, and my body was flung out of the car. I hit the pavement with my face, accounting for the many fractures I sustained. Much later, I could recall images immediately following the accident that are rather confusing and disturbing, including someone kicking me as I lay on the asphalt. I'm not clear on that detail, but what is clear is that Heathen had wrong intentions toward me. Had he planned on raping me? No doubt he had wanted to do me harm and ended up doing just that. He drugged me and put me in severe danger behind the wheel of my car. And, because of him, my appearance and, in fact, my whole life was changed in an instant.

Is this the end?

Several family members rushed to the hospital in San Antonio when they learned of my accident. My mom, however, was living in California at the time. One of my cousins called to tell her the news that every mother fears: "There's been a terrible accident. You need to get out here so you can say your goodbyes." When my mom arrived and saw me lying there she almost fainted. I looked nothing like her daughter--she couldn't believe it was me. My face was bashed in. I was hooked up to machines. This had to be a mistake!

She asked the nurse where she could find Linda Ruiz, and the nurse confirmed that the person lying there with the disfigured face was, indeed, her daughter. I was unrecognizable. Later, the doctors asked my mom for a picture of me so they could see what I looked like before the accident. The difference was so staggering that I was denied access to a mirror. Everyone thought it would be better not to let me see what I looked like. My appearance--the severe damage to my face--would be too much for me to handle.

I stayed in that hospital for nearly three months, undergoing surgery on my face, including my eyes. I went through invasive and often painful treatments, and spent day after day (after day ...) in the four walls of a hospital room, lying in bed. My jaw was wired shut and two holes were drilled into my skull to hold my jaw in place, which meant I could only take in liquids. My upper front teeth had been knocked out and there remained a trach in my throat. Due to the many fractures in my face, I was told I would probably never be able to smell or taste again. Also, doctors warned me that I would probably lose the use of my right hand due to the injuries in my wrist. This news was devastating to me. I was a young woman in my twenties with a whole life ahead of me and this is how I would have to live it? That thought overwhelmed me (by God's grace, the doctors' predictions did not come to pass. I still feel some pain in my wrist if I move it a certain way, but I have full use of my right hand and I can taste and smell just fine). The pain I felt physically throughout my body and the emotional pain that accompanied it was 24/7. I was living a nightmare.

Though I was receiving care in the hospital, at times I didn't feel well-cared for. More than once when the nurses came in to clean out my trach, for example, they were less than gentle and seemed to be in a hurry. They'd wiggle it around, adjusting it roughly as I would writhe in pain. I know they were doing their job and they had other patients to attend to, but a measure of gentleness and compassion would have been a huge help to me.

Once after using a bedpan (my "new normal"), I accidentally peed on myself. A nurse came to my room to change the sheets and give me a fresh gown. But instead of finishing the job, I was left through the night naked on the bed--1 had a blanket, but no sheets and no gown. When my mom arrived in the morning she was shocked and angry to find me like that. Though she wanted to complain, she was told to be careful. An advocate is often needed for patients in the hospital, and I was thankful to have my mom, but my aunt warned that if she made the nurses mad they might take it out on me. This caused my mom to tread lightly, to be delicate with the staff, which was probably the wisest (yet at times maddening) choice.

Innocent mistakes can happen, of course--not everyone was out to mis-treat me--but I had a close call that would have been a terrible mistake had it not been caught. One morning, I was woken up by a nurse who told me she was taking me to surgery. I was shocked, but I couldn't dialogue with her with the trach down my throat. I wanted to scream, "What the heck is going on? I just had surgery a few days ago!" Instead the nurse and I had a "conversation" with me scribbling words on a notepad, but she either wasn't understanding me or wasn"t believing that I was telling the truth. After going back and forth for what seemed like forever she did some research and finally realized she had the wrong patient! It turned out that there was another person in the hospital with my same name who had been in an accident and was scheduled for a similar surgery. Though I was bedridden in the hospital, apparently I had to stay on my toes! This is just another example of how the hospital didn't always feel like the safest place to me.

From the scene of the accident to my hospital experience and well be-yond, what took place on July 4th was life-altering. But this wasn't my first injury. As a young child, I once ran away from my grandfather when we were in a store together. I was mad because he wouldn't buy me the toy I wanted so I ran out of the store, into the street, and was hit by a car. The driver was drunk. Then there was that time I dumped a bucket of boiling water being used to wash our clothes. My side was burned as a result. Though the burns healed, I was left with scars as a reminder of the incident. These accidents in my younger days affected me in-and-of themselves. Perhaps, though, in a small way they served to toughen me and make me strong enough to go through this major accident as a young adult. Whether or not that's the case, somehow I was given the strength to endure.

I look back at my time in that San Antonio hospital and I'm grateful that the doctors there did, indeed, "bother with me." In response to their efforts, I fought for life and healing the best I could. Those months in the hospital were grueling and there would be more miserable months ahead, but I must have believed deep inside me that I am *worth the bother*. Heathen didn't hold the power. He couldn't take away my value as a person. I was and continue to be worth the bother. And no matter what challenges you are facing in this life--at the hands of someone evil, or by your own mistakes, or by some unfortunate circumstances that are out of your control--YOU are worth the bother, too. So...fight for life and healing.

An Awful, Long Road Ahead

"What doesn't kill you makes you stronger..."

It's not like I left the hospital whole, healed, and ready for normal life--not by a long shot! Though I was finally well enough to check out of the hospital, I still had a fight ahead of me. It would be a long time, and too many appointments to count, before I would feel and look well enough to enter the world again. It was obvious that I needed a lot of help in the process so I left Texas and went back to Oceanside, California where I had spent much of my early childhood and moved back in with my mom. She was a huge help to me, but it was an adjustment for both of us. She had work and my much younger siblings to raise on top of caring for me. And though I was thankful to be with her, moving back home was another change in my life. I had already launched from home and had a life in Texas. My accident, however, caused a domino effect in my world--one thing after another toppled over: my independence, appearance, relationships, self-esteem ... everything changed.

I had undergone surgery at the hospital in San Antonio, but the bulk of my surgeries (including orthodontic surgeries) would take place in California. During this time, I became a regular patient of an outstanding plastic surgeon named Dr. Kellis. He skillfully put my face back together, though, truthfully, it would never be the same. I had too much damage done to my face to be fully restored. I remember thumbing through a binder he had in his waiting room and viewing pictures of before-and-after faces. It made me sick to look at the photos as the reality of how disfigured I was soaked in. Apparently it made others sick as well as more than once I was

greeted with mortified stares and hurtful comments whispered loud enough for me to hear when I'd enter the waiting room. I was once referred to as a "monster." Incidences like this cut deep, wreaking havoc on my self-esteem.

An even greater emotional pain was hatched inside of me when I realized that some of my family members no longer accepted me. At one point, when I was further along in my healing, I moved from my mom's house to an aunt's place. There my cousins, who, pre-accident, used to include me in their weekend activities, were now no longer inviting me to join them. It was obvious that my appearance was an embarrassment to them. It's awful to feel unwanted and rejected, especially by people you love and thought loved you. In all this, I climbed into a hole of depression.

What helped me out of that hole was my bent towards work. I like being busy and working hard. Meaningful activity can help chase the blues away. So after a long recovery period from the accident and the surgeries that followed (I wasn't fully recovered, but I'd made significant progress) I landed a job not far from where I was living in Oceanside. I first got a position with a company that made airplane parts, then I moved on to another company and was trained to work on computer circuit boards. It was a challenge for me, but I was trained well, and I enjoyed the work. With all the injuries I survived, praise God I didn't suffer any brain damage. I stuck with this work and added other jobs. I was working day and night with the goal of saving enough money to move back to San Antonio.

Though in some respects I was a California girl having spent much of my childhood there, I was born in Texas and had lived there a while. It seemed like I should go back. Texas was in my blood, I guess. Besides, my past friendships in California were no longer the same. People had moved on and those who stayed (cousins and others) had distanced themselves from me.

2
A LOOK BACK AT CHILDHOOD
From Texas

I 've never been one to research my genealogy, but what I do know is that I'm mostly Mexican-American (some debate that it should be called "American-Mexican") and also part Native American. I was born in Texas in the late 50's, the oldest of seven children. I didn't live out too much of my childhood in Texas, but the short time I was there as a young girl I remember spending time with my grandfather. And I do believe I was his favorite! He made me feel as if I was his "number one," which is a sweet memory for me. We spent a lot of time together, and he spoiled me (except for that day when he wouldn't buy me the toy I wanted)! When we'd visit him as I got older, this special relationship continued, and I'm thankful for it.

To California

When I was still preschool age, Mom left for California to find work, and I stayed with my grandfather and some aunts and uncles until she returned for me. We then migrated from San Antonio to Oceanside, California, a coastal town outside of San Diego. My mom was a single mother for part of this time (she later met the man who would become my step-father and I would gain three younger sisters who I adore). Mom was also a hard worker and a good provider. She was employed by a packing company and worked from seven in the morning until eleven at night most days, packing tomatoes in the warehouse. I so admire my mom for all she did to put food on the table and keep a roof over our heads. She set a great example for me, and I'm sure work ethic came from her.

I liked living in Oceanside. It was a small town in many ways, and our entertainment was simple pleasures. It wasn't a simple time in the world, however. The 60s and 70s were a time of debate and great emotion with the Vietnam War growing in controversy. The headquarters for the MDM ("Movement for a Democratic Military") was established in our quaint town, which brought anti-war activist Jane Fonda to the area several times. The famous Patty Hearst scandal later took place in 1974. But my friends and I were too young to be much concerned over these things. Our lives revolved around hanging out at the beach, going to the movies or skating at the rink, and spending time and money at the arcade. The Marine Corps Base Camp Pendleton is located in Oceanside and the "jarheads," as we called the marines, would often hang out at the arcade, too, playing a part in the background of my growing up years. My childhood wasn't perfect (is anyone's?), but it was good, and I enjoyed life in Oceanside.

San Antonio ... Once Again

Upon finishing my junior year in high school, however, my mom decided to move the family back to San Antonio. I was mad over this decision. Leaving my high school and especially the friends I had grown up with since kindergarten and attending a new school in a different state made me feel angry and lost. I hated not knowing anyone and couldn't seem to find my people and make friends. I was miserable. As a result, I frequently got into trouble and often skipped school. Yet, I can now look back at this challenging time as well and recognize how it helped shape me and toughen me for what I would contend with later. Adversity can give birth to strength if you let it.

Before, when I was attending high school in California, I had planned on graduating and going on to college or pursuing a career in the military (perhaps I'd been influenced by those jarheads at the arcade in Oceanside), but my mom was adamantly against me going into the service. Then, as I went through so many challenges my senior year in Texas, I no longer knew what I wanted to do. My motivation for college had dwindled. I ended up getting a job at an Olan Mills Portrait Studio and later worked at McDonald's, but these jobs weren't for me and, besides, I needed to make more money than what they offered. Then one day I ran into acquaintance who told me about a job she got from the Labor Union. This piqued my interest so I headed over to the Union see about work opportunities.

Approaching the receptionist at the front desk, I was immediately told that they weren't hiring. I hadn't even opened my mouth yet to ask! The receptionist somehow knew what I was there for and stopped me before I could get the words out. But as I turned to leave and was heading out the door a man who was a Union representative asked me how tall I was. "Five six," I told him. He then yelled over to the receptionist, "Sign her up!" *What? What is happening?* He must have seen something in me that made him feel I would be a good labor worker. Or, perhaps, he simply felt that I should be given a chance. For whatever reason, I was thrilled by this turn of events and more than a little shocked at how it came to be. I knew I was being handed an opportunity, and I was going to take advantage of it.

That was the beginning of my work in the painting industry and the beginning of a long, challenging road in this "man's world" of construction. I was bound and determined, however, to prove from day one that I could hold my own, though my resolve would be tested over and over.

3

A FRESH COAT OF PAINT

Starting Over

"Oh, my friend, it's not what they take away from you that counts. It's what you do with what you have left." -Hurbert Humphrey

When I went to my mom's in California in order to heal after my accident, then worked on computer circuit boards and other jobs in Oceanside, I finally was able to save enough to move back to San Antonio. Yes, my fractured bones had healed, and I had recovered from my several surgeries (it took about three years), but I was returning to Texas scarred--physically and emotionally. Still, even after all I had gone through at the hands of Heathen and the daily injustices I was put through on job sites before my accident, I was a painter. I had been trained as a painter, and I had earned my stripes.

Becoming a painter is more than just picking up a brush. Once I joined the Union, I learned a great deal on the job while an apprentice, but I also was required to attend school for four hours every Tuesday for three years. If I didn't get to class, I couldn't work the next day. I jumped through all the hoops and learned my trade. Having fully paid my dues through hard labor, and school before my accident, I now wanted back in. I wanted to start painting again. And getting back in the game after being out of it for a few years, I knew more about what to expect. Continuing to work on computer circuit boards would have been an easier road, no doubt! But I felt it was time for me to get onto a construction site and start again.

Working in a Man's World --
(And Getting "Schooled")

From day one on my first job site (before ever meeting Heathen, before my accident), after being signed on to become an apprentice, I learned that working as a painter would be hard labor (you begin as an apprentice before you can become a journeyman painter in the construction trade). Before I got the job, I really knew nothing about this line of work and, in fact, when a person starts out, he/she doesn't do any actual painting.

As an apprentice you're a "gopher"--retrieving, delivering and doing whatever the painters tell you to. Then you learn to sand, caulk, and do a lot of clean up, etc. Not only is the work itself extremely physical, requiring strength (a five-gallon bucket of paint weighs over 50 pounds and there's a great deal of additional equipment to haul), but that's only part of the challenge. I also learned within seconds of walking onto my first job that most of my co-workers were real asses. They made it clear that I wasn't welcome and the harsh reality of that required strength, too. Emotional strength.

I went to work day in and day out--at this job and the many others that would follow--at what I called the "boys' club," (even getting to work each day took resolve as I traveled by bus which had its own challenges). I knew full well that my co-workers (primarily Hispanic men) didn't think a woman had any business working on construction sites and they were out to "school" me and put me in my place. They resented my presence and many of them let me know every chance they got. It was their goal to try to make it as tough as they could for me so that I'd give up and quit. Their cruelty wore me down emotionally, but I didn't run away. I wouldn't quit. And, in fact, I quickly developed a stubborn will to stick with it.

On my first day as a helper, I was told to haul two five-gallon cans of water up three flights of stairs (no elevator). I did this over and over all day in addition to other tasks--whatever the painters demanded of me--and I did it with them smirking behind my back and sometimes openly calling me names. I wasn't permitted to take the breaks that I was due. I had to keep working. It was hard to breathe. Yet I survived and returned the next day sore and tired but fully determined to do this work.

After I proved to my co-workers that they couldn't get rid of me, I earned a measure of respect and that helped settle down some of the harassment and they eased up. After a while some started to invite me to grab a beer after work or eat lunch with them. This felt like a huge accomplishment. I had proved myself and won a few over.

That first job lasted about three months. From there, however, I frequently had to go through the whole routine again and fight to gain the men's respect and acceptance at each new job site. Sometimes I would never be accepted. I'd be shunned and left out. If a few were going to the store on a break, and I asked to come along, they'd tell me there was no room for me. If I needed a lift at the end of the day, I'd be told no one was going my way. It was all emotionally and mentally exhausting. Anger bubbled up inside me, and I had to go to battle with the depression and anxiety that accompanied it. Still, there were some decent guys that would emerge once I proved myself, and they'd treat me with more kindness. I will always be thankful for them.

In my attempt to win over the bulk of these men, full of their own macho pride, I learned that it wasn't enough to prove I was a good worker, though that's why I was there--to work. As I stayed in this business, I grew to feel that I had to play at their game from time to time. I couldn't let my guard down. At times, though, I compromised what I knew was right, and I did and said things I wish I hadn't. Looking back to those earlier days, I'd do some things differently, no doubt. But I learned from my mistakes, and I've learned not to dwell on past decisions. That's the only way to move forward.

Coming back to the construction world and facing its challenges again after all I had been through due to my accident was in many ways a "starting over" season. For the most part I felt ready for it, but there were plenty of days that I'd wonder what the heck I was thinking getting back into this "man's world."

4

A TARGET ON MY BACK

I Could Tell You a Hundred Stories...

Returning to my work as a painter after my accident, I came back on the scene a little older and a little wiser, but still young and relatively inexperienced compared with many of the men in the business. After the accident, I continued to struggle with significant and growing negative self-esteem issues. My face looked different, of course, after all my injuries and surgeries. Many of the guys I had worked with before the accident were still in the business and they were pretty good to me, but there were others who weren't.

I knew I was a good painter by this time, but I found myself in a non-stop battle to constantly prove myself I always felt as if I had a target on my back with some of these guys. As a result, I lived in survival mode. This led me more than once to compromise what I knew was right and allow some evil men to take advantage of me. Unfortunately, I felt at the time that I had to allow or go along with certain things just to survive. This meant I put up with a lot of crap. Too much. And I paid a price for it.

Perhaps you've found yourself in a similar situation--once or multiple times. If the Me Too Movement had been established whe I had started out in the construction trade, it could have been a whole different ball game for me. Today women are not only more aware of their rights, but a greater number have found their voice in fighting for those rights. I was convinced that I couldn't be thought of as a complainer and I had to just suck up mistreatment and even sexual abuse. I'm sure I would have been more vocal about what I was going through had I had the example and backing of such a movement. I'm speaking out now by way of this book because of my goal to help and inspire others who are suffering from abuse. I want women to know they have the power to fend it off.

This book would be too heavy to lift if I were to record all the abusive incidents that happened to me over the years in this "man's world." I hope that's not your reality, but if you've suffered, read on. You're not alone.

Just Let Me Do my Job

Abuse occurred in both seemingly small as well as in large, life-altering ways--many times over. And there were many brands of it: sometimes it was sexual, often it was verbal and it also came in the form of withholding that which I was due. At times, I was not given the training I needed to advance. Training is part of being an apprentice. But instead of spending the time to train me, sometimes I'd be ignored and left to figure things out for myself. Some of the guys I worked with had a lot to offer--they were the old-timers and who knew a great deal that they could teach me. I'm a quick learner! But they were afraid that the younger workers would become so skilled that they'd take over their jobs and having a younger worker who was female play a part in that was over the top for them. As a result, I had to fight to learn some things that were best learned on the job site.

Over time, all this crap added up and became destructive in ways that are hard to measure. I would often be at work and think "Just let me do my job!" Back then, and to this day, when I'm at work, I'm there to work. I'm not there to have to put up with abuse or play games. When a work environment is toxic, a person can't perform at their best level. I worked much of my time in toxic environments and it took a toll on me in every way. How can it not? This continued to be my experience for years.

To be honest, it's painful to put into words what I went through at the hand of Heathen and other evil men. I don't like to talk about it. But as I reveal to you a few incidences of some of the abuse I experienced, I do so for your sake--not to entertain you, but to hopefully empower you. For a time, I resolved myself as a female in the construction trade, to accept what was happening to me as "part of the journey." Don't let this be your journey no matter what career you're in or what things are like at home. Abuse should never be a part of anyone's journey! You and me both--we were made for more than abuse. We must call out the creeps and say, "No!"

5
CALLING OUT (SOME OF) THE CREEPS

Ted--One of the Creeps

I remember seeing Ted on one of the job sites I was on before my accident, but I had never had any interaction with him. Returning now to construction, I found myself working on the same crew as Ted. I had no prior opinion of this guy since I had never talked with him before, but as, I began working directly with him, it was obvious that he was full of hate, and he would bring me trouble. As I worked one with the crew, he'd instruct co-workers to "Call the lesbian and tell her to come help you." Ted had no filter and calling me lesbian and referring to me as puta ("whore" in Spanish) happened throughout the day. He didn't care if I heard, of course, because Ted was a bully. He didn't know me, and he had no reason to harass me, but when I walked on the job site it seemed that I was, in his eyes, someone to conquer and destroy, and he used every tactic and opportunity to do that.

Like a twelve-year-old junior high bully, he did what he could to embarrass and belittle me in front of the crew. This was Ted's game. For example, one day as I went to an empty floor of the multi-floor building we were working on, I got off the elevator to where the rest of the crew was eating their lunch. I dared enter the area to have my own lunch and get a break, which I deserved like everyone else. I wasn't welcome there at the "boys' club" but I had earned my lunch break, and I refused to hide away. So I took a spot on the floor as the group layed around, resting, eating, and joking with each other. I kept my distance and, essentially, ate my lunch alone (can you picture it? I'm the only woman there and throughout the day I've already been harassed and verbally abused. Imagine how uncomfortable I felt eating my lunch next to these guys, but this was how it was. I didn't feel like I could change anything).

When I finished my lunch, I got up to leave and was hit by something. Ted had thrown ice at me. *Really? Why is this guy such an ass?* The men on "Team Ted" thought this was hilarious and had a laugh at my expense. I couldn't win in this situation. If I ignored it, he'd keep on. If I yelled at him, he'd get what he wanted--a fight. Daily, I had to navigate this sort of thing. It was exhausting and the anxiety it produced in me grew over time. With guys like Ted, I never knew how far things would go. I was afraid of him.

Ted's step-father also worked on the crew and apparently harassing women ran in the family. Though Manuel wasn't verbally abusive, I discovered that working near him was not safe. While assisting him as he sprayed down some doors with lacquer one day, his knuckles brushed against my breasts. I can see how this happening once could be an accident, but Manuel clearly knew what he was doing and did it several times.

After a while Ted's abuse turned sexual as well. Before it took place, I had asked him one day what I had to do to get him to stop hating me so much. From there he started taking advantage of me until he finally forced me to have sex with him. I hated myself for being a victim like that, but I was also in survival mode. I needed my job, and I felt that I needed him to stop messing with me at work. I was hurting. Day in and day out, punching the time clock and knowing I should expect disrespect and harassment on several levels was killing me. All this because I was a woman working in a man's world? How pathetic is that? I felt like I had nowhere to turn and so I'd just have to do what I had to do. I hated it, but I was trapped, and it felt unsafe at the time to blow the whistle on Ted. If I snitched, I feared that I'd pay a higher price.

If you're caught in a similar way of thinking, let me stop you right now. You do NOT have to put up with such crap. Call the perpetrator out before he has the opportunity to do any more harm to you. Blow the damn whistle and put a stop to things. There are resources available to you now that I didn't have back then, or at least that I was aware of.

After a while, things settled down with Ted so I let it go. I shouldn't have. The "effects" of Ted damaged me further than I had already been damaged. What ensued in me was a victim mentality which perpetuated more incidences of abuse. I'm not saying these things were my fault--I clearly was a victim--but I had rights and strength I didn't realize I had.

The Creep that was Clay

And then there was Clay. He would prove to be one of the worst. By this time the Painter's Union had relocated outside my area and our jobs became what is referred to as "open shop," which meant I was no longer earning Union wages. So I decided to look for other work and ended up finding a job I would deeply regret. The owner of the company was named Clay and his office, oddly enough, was located in the kitchen of his house. It soon became a bad situation working for Clay, but I didn't realize how twisted it was right away, or maybe I just allowed things because I had it in my head that I needed this job. To add to that, I was young, had been taken advantage of before, and had such a low self-esteem after the accident that I didn't embrace my worth.

So when I came to work for Clay I was a prime target for him. He was a master manipulator. He was a widower, and he began confiding in me, preying on my emotions. For a while I felt sorry for him. He'd cry in front of me and share about his sorrow over his wife's passing. He made me believe we were friends at first, and he'd ask little favors of me like making him drinks, cleaning his house, running errands. I felt I had to do what he wanted so I could keep my job. He acted as if he was taking me under his wing by teaching me to read blueprints and, of course, he was supplying me with some painting jobs. Then he began touching me and forcing me to touch him. It was gross. I felt disgusted but I also felt worthless and didn't stand up for myself with force. I'd tell him that I didn't feel comfortable being there with him like that, but he was threatening. Finally, he raped me. I got pregnant and had an abortion.

Even then Clay would say to me, "Do you want this job? Then do what I'm telling you to do." He had me brainwashed that I could do no better than him and I was in need of the work. I was in my late twenties by this time. I supported myself. I was also spending too much of my money at times on drugs and alcohol once the weekend would come around and I'd gotten paid. I was ashamed of this, too, and I hid it the best I could from my family. I was just in so much pain from Clay; from my life. I was trying to anesthetize it. Clay would tell me that no one would hire me, and I was lucky to be working for him. But the truth was, I felt cursed to be working for him. He regularly cheated me (and some other employees). I didn't get paid for my drive time even when I had to drive a couple of hours to get to a site. He didn't reimburse me for gas, and I wouldn't always get paid for my full hours on the job.

These types of abuses beat me down and my self-esteem pummeled further. To this day I can't fully put into words how much anguish Clay put me through and how disgusting he made me feel. He was vile. It makes me sick to remember this gross old man kissing me with his whiskers and the stench of his breath. Yet my self esteem was in the toilet so deep that I put up with his abuse. It was all such an ugly thing. Until finally, one glorious day, I woke up. *Enough!* That day he had summoned me over to him and started touching my breasts over my clothes, and I snapped. "I'm not here for that," I told him. He said, "Well then, guess I don't have any more work for you." I walked out his door, a free woman at last.

There were a couple of other female employees that worked for Clay who he had victimized as well. I was able to summon some courage with their support and, together, we put in a complaint with the labor board. Clay, however, had a good lawyer and the labor board didn't do much--these guys unlawfully protected each other. Eventually we were accused of lying and going after Clay for unfair retribution. Our case ended up going nowhere and we remained unemployed. The whole situation left me with not only no sense of justice, but also a deep sense of shame at what had taken place. I had allowed Clay to take advantage of me on every level for over two years. I found out that his adult children knew much of what was going on during that time I worked for Clay. Although they felt bad about it, they did nothing to stop the abuse. Years after I left the company I found out that Clay had put a gun to his head and committed suicide. In weird way, I suppose, I received justice, but it didn't really help.

And Then There was "Kevin"

I have worked with over a thousand guys throughout my years in the painting industry and I remember a friend making a comment to me that it must be "heaven" working with all those men. She couldn't have been more wrong! I let her know the truth: more often than not, it was more like hell. I worked with piranhas. And I often got bit.

Kevin was a piranha that I especially had to look out for. I was put in his path years after I had worked with Clay. I had a good amount of experience by this time. My work was being acknowledged, and I began to grow in confidence--I had started to find my voice again. I had proven myself as a painter, and I was finally working with a good boss. His name was Fred (more on him later), and he eventually made me a foreman so I was in charge of running jobs for him. At first, because he had been hurt at work, Kevin was on the job site as a "gopher" (before that he had been a painter). Then, once he was able to paint again, he started to move up the ranks and became one of Fred's Project Managers, which meant that I regularly had to work with him. He went from being a gopher to a snake, and he grew to be a huge menace in my life.

As a foreman, I would record information about my various projects, documenting it in a book. I also began documenting the incidences of harassment and situations that happened at work. My entries on Kevin took up much of the book! I had a lot of dirt on him. He spent a lot of time and energy making every effort to harass me and make life miserable and much of it was put down in writing.

Once Kevin sent me a picture of himself on the toilet, fully exposed. But more regularly, the crap I had to deal with regarding Kevin was emotional harassment and verbal abuse. He took it upon himself to spy on me, hoping to find me doing something wrong so he could call me out. He even admitted to me that he hid in the bushes one day so he could spy on me to see what time I got in and to make sure that I wrote down the correct time on my time card. He wanted to get me fired so he kept tabs on me hoping to catch me doing something wrong so he could rat me out. He must have used up a lot of energy out of his hate for me!

Once on a Friday I did end up leaving a job site a few minutes early and Kevin discovered I was gone. I was used to Kevin's name calling and him cussing me out. He referred to me as "that f*n bitch," among other things. That Friday when I clocked out a little early, witnesses told me that Kevin was screaming my name (the name he called me) over and over, asking "Where is that F*n bitch?" I can just picture his face turning red and the steam coming out of his ears like a cartoon character, though there was nothing comical about him. And that following Monday morning when I returned to work, he continued his rampage to my face.

Of course his outbursts were always public, embarrassing, and degrading, and this one was over the top. In this way he bullied and intimidated me on a regular basis. On that day, though, I had had enough. He went on and on about me leaving that Friday, spewing insults at me, and I cussed back at him. He had me so riled and frustrated that I threw down the mud pan I was using. I didn't throw it at him--it never touched him--but this set him off even more! I had to get away from him so I stormed off, but Kevin followed me out of the building, screaming at me. I called Fred and told him what was going on (I was in tears by this point), but Kevin later wrote me up for the incident, citing that I threw a mud pan at him. The day this all went down he was so out of control that he got kicked off the job site!

Others knew what I had to put up with when it came to Kevin, but I didn't get much help or support. The "boys' club" remained intact and because Fred was rarely on site, he didn't see the way it was firsthand. But when things like this would happen, I'd document it in my book. Initially I wasn't planning on filing charges against Kevin, but I knew if I changed my mind I had everything recorded, and I had plenty of witnesses. (Later the issue of filing charges on Kevin was brought up. I was told that I had enough evidence against him--there was even video from one of the sites--but I was also advised to consider the fact that Kevin had a family to feed. Causing trouble for him would make it hard on his wife and kids. The boys' club strikes again.) To drive me even crazier, Kevin's moods could switch on a dime. At times he would act civil toward me, even friendly, and then his tune would change. For instance, he'd tell me to let him know if I needed something. But then when I did ask for water or ice on a hot day, for example, he'd deny my request. "I'm not your f*n slave," he'd tell me. "Get it yourself."

One day, when he was ranting about something, I confronted him. "What the hell is wrong with you?" I asked. "You're angry so often."

He admitted that someone else had just made him mad, and he was taking it out on me. He also acknowledged that it wasn't right. But the truth was, Kevin was intimidated by me. He knew that I knew my job well, and he didn't like the fact that Fred trusted me and put me in charge of some things. Me, a woman. The audacity!

I tried to make peace with Kevin. Lord knows I tried. I wasn't out to make enemies, and I didn't want to be the snitch who got guys in trouble. I really just wanted to be accepted and left alone to do my work. So I went out of my way to try and befriend Kevin--in a right way (and thankfully though his abuse was damaging, he didn't harm me physically/ sexually). I'd offer to loan him money when he needed some for lunch. One weekend I made him enchiladas, and my mom made him tortillas and salsa. This was a gesture toward friendship, a way of calling a truce. He accepted the food and no doubt enjoyed it, but by Monday morning, when I was back at work, he was back to cussing me out about something.

I couldn't win this guy over, and I was sick of trying. Not only that, but the environment that I faced every day was throwing me further into depression. This began to evoke debilitating anxiety in me and I found it harder and harder to make it into work. Though I had gained Fred's trust and was given responsibility, I was struggling to do my job. One day

I discovered that my book--the one I used to document abuses and other incidences at work--was stolen from where I had locked it up. Only one other guy had the key and I'm sure he helped Kevin to steal my book. I never got it back.

There Were Others...

I've highlighted a few of the creeps I've had to endure to make it in this business, but there are many, many more! Harassment against women is deeply ingrained in the construction world. Whether it's due in part to the ethnic culture of so many of the men who work in this field, or the fact that there are barely any women in this field so, somehow, the men feel justified to harass, I'm not entirely sure. Neither reason, though, is an excuse. What I do know is that the men feed off each other. Most don't have the integrity or the balls to stand up for someone they see is being harassed. At least that has been my unfortunate experience for nearly 40 years.

In what work environment is harassment considered okay? Nowhere! But in the construction world these things happened too often. Once I had a co-worker open a Playboy Magazine in front of me. Seeing my disgust, he went a step further and started describing what he would do to the woman in the picture if he had the chance. Another time someone threw a clay penis at me. This was life on the job. No wonder my depression and anxiety enveloped me.

Still, I evolved as a worker and oversaw different teams of guys at various jobs. There were times I'd call security if I felt things got out of hand, but of course that was rare. I learned to handle things on my own, and I'd let guys know that I refused to take their crap. Once I did take someone to court over an incident, and I was awarded $2500 from that case. It was a small amount, but it helped send the message that I wasn't one to mess with anymore. Little by little I found my voice, despite my past experience that still pained me.

6

THE DIFFERENCE RESPECT MAKES

The Blessing of Fred

From my accident at the hand of Heathen that left me disfigured, to what I suffered due to Ted, Clay, Kevin, and many others in between on each job site I ever stepped foot on, the negative experiences piled on top of me and weighed me down. But I can't deny that there have been some positive experiences as well, and I'd be remiss if I didn't turn a spotlight on one of the good guys in my life that gifted me with a dose of graciousness. His name is Fred.

I recently called this former boss to let him know how much I truly appreciate him. He deserves a big "thank you," for all he did for me. Because of Fred I made it through. He helped me to grow personally and professionally. He stuck with me until he wisely let me loose. He was a blessing and ultimately helped push me into starting my own business.

When I first met Fred it was on the heels of working for Clay. I was wrongly conditioned to believe at that time that I was worthless and that in order for me to be hired I would need to do whatever it took. It was a twisted way of thinking, but when your self-esteem is as unhealthy as mine was, it's how you think. My mind had been polluted, and I was deeply hurting. But Fred let me know from day one that I wasn't being hired to wash his car or clean his office (I had offered to do those things). "You're here to paint," he said. And he put me to work.

Fred saw that I did good work as a painter and after a while he gave me more responsibilities on job sites. That alone was a confidence booster! If there was a conflict between me and one of the workers that I let him know about, he generally took my side because he trusted me. He was for me. He was also patient. He cut me more slack than most bosses ever would, which I respect and appreciate him for to this day.

I worked for Fred off and on for about fourteen years. I say, "off and on" because there were times that my depression and anxiety overtook me, and I'd walk off a job site and go home (Kevin's treatment of me was more often than not the reason). For a while, I was struggling so much with my mental and emotional health that Fred couldn't count on me. He'd call me the night before and say, "I need you to come to work tomorrow--just get to the job site in the morning."

"Yes, sir," I'd tell him. "I'll be there."

The next morning I'd get ready for work and drive to the site, but when I'd arrive I couldn't get out of the car. I was in such a bad place emotionally that I count't shake it. Just being at the site caused so much anxiety to bubble up, I was paralyzed. So I'd turn the car around and drive home, leaving Fred in the lurch and feeling guilty and defeated. The culmination of too many hurts and regrets, too much pain and fear in my life for so long engulfed me. I was in a pit of despair. Still, Fred would give me a second, third, fourth chance...Some days, during that time period, I was able to summon the strength and courage to get to work and stay there. When I did, I worked hard for Fred.

Once, to assure I made it to work, he sent another co-worker to come get me and escort me to the job site! That was a bit embarrassing, but it did show that I was worth the bother--Fred saw value in me and made the effort to have me at work which, in turn, not only benefited him, but helped me.

Fred had his limits, though, and one day he finally told me he felt it was time we "parted ways." It was understandable. He needed to be able to count on me and, during that season of depression, he couldn't. But when he cut ties like that, I was devastated. The fighter in me emerged, and I had a turnaround. I started showing up for work after that and he kept me on.

Overall, I worked hard for Fred, and he knew it. He knew that I still had to put up with plenty of crap on job sites, but as my boss, he helped give me my dignity back and he built up my self-esteem by acknowledging my work. Once when a contractor started patronizing me by telling me what to do and how to do it, Fred let the guy know he was out of line. "You don't have to do that," he told him. "She's a painter, she knows what to do." Yes, I know what to do and Fred affirmed that--he stuck up for me.

One day, Fred even rewarded me with a truck! Having your own truck to use to store your equipment and drive to job sites is a big deal, and it meant a great deal to me to have one. This reward was a tangible, practical expression which said I was appreciated and worth it, and Fred gave it to me publicly, in front of my peers. It was a victory moment for me. That truck was not given to me as a gift; I had earned it. And I was proud of what I had accomplished.

Getting My "Color" Back

Like I mentioned earlier, I never set out to be a painter. But having been one for so many years, I know paint extremely well. It's in my blood, so to speak, and I like working with it! I know the ends and outs of it and how best to use it to transform a surface and make it beautiful and vibrant. In my life journey, which has been wrought with skyscraper-size challenges due in good measure to what I've had to put up with in this profession, I can equate painting with some of my deepest feelings.

"Fading" is a painting term I can relate to. It refers to the loss of color in paint due to exposure to the elements like sun, wind, and storms. Looking back on my journey, I've experienced severe *fading* in my life. When I think of who I used to be before I began work in construction, before my accident, etc., I can see how much it all took from me. I lost my brilliance; my color. I used to be more soft spoken and easy-going. I was more gentle and kind. But the *elements* I was hit with--being plunged day after day into a world of harsh words, my accident, having to watch my back, abuse, unaccceptance and "general" harassment--did a lot of damage, and I faded away over time. I found myself keeping my guard up, being negative. Depression and anxiety also robbed me of my vibrance. Out of defense, I became tough and, when I felt (and feel) I needed to, I became a harsher version of myself. It was my way to survive. Thankfully, as I grow older and heal from past hurts, I'm softening...though I have a ways to go! I'm in process and moving in the right direction.

"Pigment" is the solid material added to paint to give it its color. I recognize that quality pigment has been added to my life through the solid choices I've made as I've gotten older, and it has made a positive difference. One such choice was to stop running to drugs and alcohol. They only made the pain worse and the wallet lighter. Nothing good ever came from these substances and, after a while, I woke up to that truth. I became more responsible and careful with my life. Various studies have confirmed that adults, on average, make about 35,000 choices a day. Most of these choices are subconscious, like: "I think I'll go to bed now." But some are serious, important, even life-changing choices, like: "I'm not going to put up with this crap anymore!" And, "I'm going to stop doing drugs," etc. Good choices have given me back my *pigment* and that's a beautiful thing.

R.E.S.P.E.C.T. (Get it!)

Take a step back and look at your own life:

- What decisions are you making and where are they getting you?

- In what state is your self-esteem?

- Is it healthy?

- What could you do to help nurture it?

I was young and naive when I entered the male-dominated world of construction. I wasn't prepared for the effect this environment would have on me, and I allowed things back then that I would never allow now. At the time, though, my self-esteem was in an awful place which meant I was vulnerable.

If you are working in or entering a profession that feels like a boys' club, do yourself a favor and set the stage now to both earn and demand respect. (Of course this applies to many situations and all professions.) Consider these things:

- **Take your opportunities seriously.** Whatever field you are entering, show up for work with an air of professionalism and confidence, even if you're new at your job. If you don't feel confident, fake it 'til you make it. Unfortunately, there are people in this world who love to take advantage of others who come across as insecure. Don't let them smell fear.

- **Be teachable.** Being confident is not the same as being a know-it-all. Accept correction and be willing to learn.

- **Know what you're there for.** You are at work to do your job. You are not there to be someone's punching bag (verbally, physically or emotionally) or sexual play thing. Understand and recognize what harassment looks like. It is any unwelcome conduct from a boss, co-worker, customer/client, etc. Being yelled at, threatened, belittled, and ridiculed are all examples of verbal harassment. Any physical assault, sexual advances, including being exposed to pictures that are sexual in nature are all examples of harassment. You're not there for that. You don't deserve it and you don't have to put up with it.

- **Don't send mixed messages.** Laughing at dirty jokes, wearing provocative clothes, ignoring a threat, etc. are the types of things that send a message of acceptance and even participation in harassment. Since becoming a business owner, I once let a female worker go after telling her more than once to stop wearing white see-through painter's pants and then bending over in front of her male co-workers. It became obvious that she liked the attention... until she didn't and then she complained. Don't flirt with disaster. Dress and act professional and keep your message clear: "I'm here to work."

- **Know your rights. Know your worth.** If you are harassed in any way, you don't have to suck it up and "'just take it." Over and over again I was intimidated. Too often I felt as though I had to put up with harassment and abuse in order to keep my job. My lack of self-esteem kept me believing that lie. But here is a fact: today is a new day! The MeToo Movement has opened up the world's eyes to what too many women are experiencing, and men who abuse and harass women are scared, as they should be. You don't have to put up with crap. In fact, you must blow the whistle. When you do, be completely honest about the situation. Tell someone higher up what is going on and if he or she doesn't act on your behalf, go over that person's head to someone over them. You may be fearful or feel that it's not worth the hassle, but in the long run (and quite possibly in the short run), it will pay off in your favor.

Remember, it doesn't matter your age, ethnicity, socioeconomic standing, or sexual orientation. All workers--*all people*--deserve respect. I wish I would have demanded it from the beginning.

7

NOW I'M THE BOSS

If it Wasn't for Fred

"If you don't like the road you're walking, start paving another one." -Dolly Parton

I continued working for Fred, which I appreciated, but the environment on job sites, mainly due to Kevin, continued to keep an unnecessary layer of stress in my work life. It was sucking the life out of me. So, one day when I had to put up with yet another one of Kevin's antics, I walked off the job and told Fred, "I quit." The next day, a co-worker came to collect my truck. At the time it felt like a huge relief to quit, but a few days later I panicked. *What have I done?* I called Fred to tell him I'd come back to work, but he told me, "No, I think it's time we parted ways." This time he meant it. Having him refuse to take me back was extremely hard, but it soon turned out to be a real gift.

For about five years I had been thinking of starting my own painting business, and now that I was no longer with Fred, I had the push I needed to get serious. I had helped to make Fred a lot of money, and I felt like I could branch out on my own and make money for myself, but, still, I was afraid. *What if I failed?* When I stopped focusing on those possible negatives, and also stopped just dreaming about having my own business and started going after it, things began to happen.

A Little Help, Please

I had some money saved up which gave me a buffer and bought me time to figure things out. Starting a business is no small thing, and I knew I would need to have a lot of things in place to give my business a real chance to thrive. So, I reached out and asked some people in my life for help.

My family came through! They helped me get the word out and some hired me to paint for them. My sister Laura joined me in establishing the business and helped me to obtain a Minority and Women Owned Business Certification. My sister Jennifer provided practical, wise help, and my other sister, Christina, and her husband, Steven, advertised for me on Nextdoor. These things made a difference and gave me my footing[1].

Little by little I was asked to make additional bids and was given jobs which kept me busy and financially afloat. Providing quality work helped me secure repeat customers and gain referrals. A significant breakthrough came for me when I secured a commercial contract painting for Wells Fargo. I was on my way, and I loved (and still love) being my own boss, even with all the headaches that come with it.

Years before I officially started my business, I had mentioned my desire to some guys that I had worked with and for. Quite a few had told me, "If you do get out on your own, call me and I'll help." So, I reached out to them, but only one came through--a friend named Eddy. He taught me

---

1. My business--LJC Painting--by the way, was lovingly named after my dear baby sisters: L for Laura, J for Jennifer, C for Christina. I would give my life in an instant for all three of "the babies" and naming the business after them has been one way for me to show my honor and express my thankfulness.

further how to read blueprints which was a help, but Eddy had an accident and died soon after. As for the others, not one of them threw any jobs or help my way. Turns out, I didn't need them.

I Didn't Die Then,
I Refuse to Die Now

That first year of finding my footing as a business owner was a challenge, but I was determined. You must be determined to start your own business--you can't be complacent. But one added challenge continued to be me! I was still so mindful of my scars which were both physical and emotional that I felt insecure much of the time (I still hate looking in the mirror and rarely agree to have my picture taken). I had to look past my own self and the impact the accident had on my face. I also had to rise up against the effects of the abuse and harassment I had endured for so many years at the hands of co-workers and bosses. It's not easy to rise above these things, but I pressed on. I continue to press on.

One way I press on personally is to put into practice the many lessons I've learned over the years regarding what I will accept from others and what I won't. Life is one lesson after another. Sometimes we learn and relearn the same thing over and over, but, eventually, the lesson sticks.

I press on professionally by putting into action the wise business practices I've learned, and it has paid off. Paying attention to detail, taking pride in my work, hiring quality workers, having integrity, and being a woman of my word for my clients as well as my staff, and also going the extra mile for clients have all helped my business thrive. At the end of the day, if my business thrives or dies it's on me. My reputation is on the line and I work hard to protect it. I didn't physically die after my accident and I have had that same fighting spirit in regards to my business. I refused to die then and I refuse to allow my business to die now! All that I've gone through has helped me to be a strong woman...and fighter.

8

I SURVIVED...AND I KEEP ON SURVIVING

Thankful that the Doctors Did "Bother"

Those moments with me in that hospital elevator, seeing "the light," hearing the cruel words of the nurse, and all that took place before and after that scene will forever be part of my story. But I can also look back to that time and experience more than pain--I can also experience gratefulness.

I am so thankful that the doctors did bother. I'm so glad that they worked to keep me alive and helped me heal physically. I'm also convinced that God had a plan for me, and though I suffered at the hands of evil people, God is not evil. He never left me, and He is still with me. Every day that I do my work, and do it well, I give testimony to the fact that my life has purpose. I realized this well before I started my own business and, in fact, that reality is what helped me to stop doing drugs and abusing alcohol. I thought, "Jesus didn't give me another chance to abuse it!" and I started to do better. I got my act together. Looking back on my life I think, "I didn't grow up until my fifties!" But that's okay--I have grown up. And I've also come to fully believe the truth: I was and continue to be "worth the bother."

You Can Survive, Too!

My story is unique because it's mine, but I have no doubt that many other women have experienced similar things. Abuse and harassment always bring with them various degrees of feelings of worthlessness, powerlessness, and deep struggle. If you can relate, I'm so sorry, but I want you to know that you're not alone and you can survive.

We've all seen some of the cop shows, court dramas, and various hospital series on television, but I think it's time for a show about a woman working in construction. It would be a hit! It could highlight the on-going chauvinistic attitudes a woman regularly faces when she dares enter this field. A show about a woman working in construction wouldn't be realistic without telling the story of abuse and harassment that takes place in this "man's world." I sure would love to see that show--I'd tune in every week and root for the female characters! A show like that would shed some light on what goes on and expose the world to the truth about this field.

In my own way, that is why I've recorded my story in this book--to expose the truth and to help others. If you have been a victim and have gone through a life-altering challenge to some degree, I hope you've found my story to be relatable and, ultimately, inspiring. I want you to feel empowered to rise above your circumstances no matter what they are and move forward. You have a life to live--one, full of purpose and free of abuse. You too, are worth the bother.

www.ingramcontent.com/pod-product-compliance
Lightning Source LLC
Chambersburg PA
CBHW061159040426
42445CB00013B/1748